Wiley Keys to Success

# HOW TO WRITE A GREAT RESEARCH PAPER

**Beverly Ann Chin** is Professor of English, Director of the English Teaching Program, former Director of the Montana Writing Project, and a former President of the National Council of Teachers of English.

Dr. Chin is a nationally recognized leader in English language arts standards, curriculum instruction, and assessment. Many schools and states call upon her to help them develop programs in reading and writing across the curriculum. Dr. Chin has edited and written numerous books and articles in the field of English language arts. She is the author of *On Your Own: Writing* and *On Your Own: Grammar.*

Wiley Keys to Success

# How to Write a Great Research Paper

**Beverly Ann Chin, Ph.D.**
Series Consultant

WILEY

John Wiley & Sons, Inc.

**Developed, Designed and Produced by BOOK BUILDERS LLC**

Published by John Wiley & Sons, Inc., Hoboken, New Jersey
Published simultaneously in Canada

For general information about our other products and services, please contact our Customer Care Department within the United States at (800) 762-2974, outside the United States at (317) 572-3993 or fax (317) 572-4002.

Wiley also publishes its books in a variety of electronic formats. Some content that appears in print may not be available in electronic books. For more information about Wiley products, visit our web site at www.wiley.com.

*Library of Congress Cataloging-in-Publication Data:*

How to write a great research paper / Beverly Ann Chin, series editor.
  p. cm.
 Includes bibliographical references and index.
 ISBN 0-471-43154-0 (pbk. : alk. paper)
 1. Report writing—Juvenile literature. 2. Research—Juvenile literature. I. Chin, Beverly Ann.
 LB1047.3.H69 2004
808'.02—dc22

Printed in the United States of America

10 9 8 7 6 5 4 3 2 1

# Dear Students

Welcome to the **WILEY KEYS TO SUCCESS** series! The books in this series are practical guides designed to help you be a better student. Each book focuses on an important area of schoolwork, including building your vocabulary, studying and doing homework, writing research papers, taking tests, and more.

Each book contains seven chapters—the keys to helping you improve your skills as a student. As you understand and use each key, you'll find that you will enjoy learning more than ever before. As a result, you'll feel more confident in your classes and be better prepared to demonstrate your knowledge.

I invite you to use the **WILEY KEYS TO SUCCESS** series at school and at home. As you apply each key, you will open the doors to success in school as well as to many other areas of your life. Good luck, and enjoy the journey!

Beverly Ann Chin, Series Consultant
Professor of English
University of Montana, Missoula

# NOTE TO TEACHERS, LIBRARIANS, AND PARENTS

The **WILEY KEYS TO SUCCESS** series is a series of handbooks designed to help students improve their academic performance. Happily, the keys can open doors for everyone—at home, in school, at work.

Each book is an invaluable resource that offers seven simple, practical steps to mastering an important aspect of schoolwork, such as building vocabulary, studying and doing homework, taking tests, and writing research papers. We hand readers seven keys—or chapters—that show them how to increase their success as learners—a plan intended to build lifelong learning skills. Reader-friendly graphics, self-assessment questions, and comprehensive appendices provide additional information.

Helpful features scattered throughout the books include "Writing it Right," which expands on the text with charts, graphs, and models; "Inside Secret," which reveals all-important hints, rules, definitions, and even warnings; and "Ready, Set, Review," which makes it easy for students to remember key points.

**WILEY KEYS TO SUCCESS** *are designed to ensure that all students have the opportunity to experience success.* Once students know achievement, they are more likely to become independent learners, effective communicators, and critical thinkers. Many readers will want to use each guidebook by beginning with the first key and progressing systematically to the last key. Some readers will select the keys they need most and integrate what they learn with their own routines.

As educators and parents, you can encourage students to use the books in this series to assess their own strengths and weaknesses as learners. Using students' responses and your own observations of their study skills and habits, you can help students develop positive attitudes, set realistic goals, form successful schedules, organize materials, and monitor their own academic progress. In addition, you can discuss how adults use similar study strategies and communication skills in their personal and professional lives.

We hope you and your students will enjoy the **WILEY KEYS TO SUCCESS** series. We think readers will turn to these resources time and time again. By showing students how to achieve everyday success, we help children grow into responsible, independent young adults who value their education—and into adults who value learning throughout their lives.

Beverly Ann Chin, Series Consultant
Professor of English
University of Montana, Missoula

# CONTENTS

# INTRODUCTION

## What Is a Research Paper and

## What Do You Gain by Writing One?

So you have to write a research paper? If this assignment makes you feel nervous or overwhelmed, you may simply be feeling a fear of the unknown. Calm down! Take it easy! Let's begin by discussing just what a research paper is. Once you know more about what you want to do, the chances are it won't seem so daunting.

A research paper is a piece of writing that provides information about a particular topic that you've researched. It's not as simple as writing a paper about your summer vacation, because you don't have to do research to find out about your own personal experience. On the other hand, a paper about a topic such as dolphins, cave paintings, ancient civilizations, or the history of a particular sport does qualify as a research paper. These are topics about which you, yourself, are not an expert, but that you can learn about by reading the work of experts—in other words, by doing research. Then you can communicate in writing what you have learned. Ideally, you will do that in a way that is clear and interesting.

If you're concerned that you won't know how to go about writing a research paper, don't worry. This book is here to help you write a great research paper. It makes writing your paper easy, because it leads you through the whole process every step of the way. This book promises to give you plenty of help—in a way that's easy to understand—so you'll do just fine.

Before we get started, we should answer a question many students ask about research papers: "What's the point? What will I gain from doing this?" One answer is that you'll gain experience in writing research papers! This may sound silly, but it's not. Chances are, you'll have to do this more than once—and probably a lot as you get older!—so after you've done it the first time, it will get a lot easier. But you'll gain more than that.

You'll learn a great deal about a topic that interests you. You'll start out knowing only a little about that topic and end up an expert in your own right. And perhaps most importantly, you'll learn how to do research. This is a skill you'll use all your life. It's been said that the mark of a good education is not how much you know, but how good you are at finding out what you need to know. Clearly, knowing how to do research is an important skill to have.

Finally, you'll gain the experience of taking on a task, seeing it through to the end, and being proud of your accomplishment. After you've completed your paper, you'll know just how rewarding this can be.

# FIND A TOPIC

✓ **Which Topics Work (and Which Ones Don't)**

✓ **The Right Topic for You**

✓ **Narrow Your Topic**

✓ **Schedule Your Work**

*Writing a research paper is a big job. However, you can make it easier by breaking it into smaller parts. The place to start is by answering the question, "What's it all about?"*

If your teacher has already chosen a topic, your first job has been done for you. But many teachers leave this job—or at least part of it—up to you. Your teacher may give you an assignment such as, "Write a research paper on any topic you choose." Or, she or he may give you a general topic but leave the specific topic up to you: "Write a research paper on a topic related to the American Revolution." You are not expected to find out everything about the American Revolution, of course. Rather, your teacher expects you to think about what you've already learned about this large, general topic and then focus on some specific part of it in your paper.

Although choosing your own topic is more work than having a topic given to you, the extra thought allows you to find a topic you're truly interested in and will enjoy learning and writing about. Try to think of it as having a world of possibilities at your fingertips.

## Which Topics Work (and Which Ones Don't)

The job of choosing a topic for a research paper is bigger than it sounds, especially if your teacher has given you free range. You can make it easier by keeping these simple guidelines in mind.

### What Interests You

Some students think that the best way to choose a topic is to find one that sounds easy. Choosing an easy topic may backfire, however, if the topic doesn't interest you all that much. Remember that you'll be living with this assignment for several days, or even weeks. Think how sorry you will be after four or five days of thinking, reading, and writing about a topic that you find boring.

What can you do if the assigned topic just doesn't grab your interest? One alternative you can try is talking with your teacher about writing your paper on a similar topic in the same subject area. First, write down an alternative "assignment" to show your teacher. Then, tell your teacher that if he or she approves, you would like to write your paper on this similar topic. (Be sure to make it clear that you are willing to do the original assignment, even if the teacher does not approve your alternative approach.) If the teacher does not approve your suggestion, he or she has a good reason for that, so try to be understanding.

Many students are surprised to find that they become more interested in a topic after they've learned more about it—even when they did not expect to enjoy it. If you're stuck with a topic that makes your eyes glaze over, try discussing the topic with others who may help you find a more interesting angle. You also might try thinking about what makes this topic interesting to other people. As you find out more, you may discover something there that interests you after all.

## What You Can Handle

Some topics are hard to handle because they are too large, or *broad*. "The American Revolution" is an example of such a topic. Seasoned scholars have written volumes on this subject, but no single person can cover every aspect of this major event in just one paper. Instead, focus on narrowing down your topic to answer favorite questions you may

have about the topic, such as "The Causes of the American Revolution" or "The Battle of Lexington and Concord."

Another example of a topic that is too broad is "Plants." The study of plants—also called *botany*—is a whole branch of science in itself. Someone who wants to write about plants, however, might pick a narrower topic such as "Carnivorous Plants" or "Plants of the Arctic." (You'll learn more about how to narrow a topic later in this chapter.)

Choosing a topic that is *too* narrow is hard to do. (Most topics—even very narrow ones—seem to get bigger as you start finding out more about them.) However, some topics can be too limiting. For example, while you could probably find plenty to say about "Cacti" and even about one particular kind of cactus, such as "The Saguaro Cactus," you might have trouble writing more than a page or so on "Comparative Heights of Saguaro Cacti." Picking a topic that's too narrow is unlikely, but watch out for it anyway.

## What You Can Find Enough Information About

Suppose you've identified a topic that you find interesting and that seems to be neither too broad nor too narrow. Before you say, "This is it!" ask yourself the question, "Can I find enough information on this topic?" For example, maybe you read the science section of your local newspaper last week and were fascinated by an article on new findings about the planet Mars. Even though that topic could be the basis of a great paper, the only information available might be the article you read and one highly technical report written by a group of space scientists.

Another pitfall is that you might choose a topic that's interesting to so few individuals (besides yourself) that only a few experts have written about it. For example, if you chose to write about your neighbor's newest invention, you would find very little written about it other than, perhaps, your neighbor's own personal writing. Either way, choosing a topic you can't find out enough about can cause you more work than you bargained for.

How can you know whether you'll be able to find enough information about a topic? This is the time to do some *preliminary research*. Start with a good encyclopedia, which you can find in the library or online. If your family owns its own encyclopedia, start there. Look up your topic to see if there is a good-sized article about it. If so, this is one sign that you can find sufficient information. Another important sign to look for is a list at the end of the article, one that includes related subjects in the encyclopedia. If you find such a list, look up some of the related subjects to see if they yield other useful information.

Next, check out your school or local library catalog. Finding at least three books about your topic is another encouraging sign. Take a little time to look through some of the books you find listed. (If you need help locating books in the library, you can ask a librarian.)

This is not the time to read a whole book or start taking notes, but you can decide now whether the available information on your topic is on the right level for you. A good way to judge the writing level of a book is by looking at the first page and then opening the book at random to pages in the middle and toward the end. By skimming several pages, you should be able to see if the book is on your level—not too easy or too hard.

Finally, log on to the Internet. Use a search engine to do a *keyword* search, with your topic as the keyword. See what comes up. Are there many Web sites? Read the descriptions of some of the available sites. Do they sound promising? Visit a few of the sites that you think might be helpful. Are they well organized and easy to follow? Do they give information you can use?

If the books and Web sites you find are too difficult or too technical, or if you don't find enough information on your topic, then the topic is probably not right for you. It's time to go back to square one and look for a new topic.

## The Right Topic for You

Choosing the topic that is right for you is crucial. By following these steps for finding a topic, you will be able to find one on which you can gather plenty of information, that you find interesting, and that is neither too broad nor too narrow.

### An Idea Web

You may have made an idea web before and referred to it as a "cluster" or an "idea map." Because a web is a way of organizing your ideas visually, it's one kind of *graphic organizer*. An idea web can be an extremely efficient tool for finding a topic that interests you. It works on the assumption that one idea leads to another.

To make an idea web, you need a blank sheet of paper that's at least $8^{1}/_{2}" \times 11"$ (the size of a standard sheet of notebook paper). Begin by drawing a circle in the middle of your paper. Then, in the circle, write the first topic you can think of, even if it's not a topic you're actually considering. As other related topics come to your mind, write them in smaller circles surrounding the original circle. Draw lines leading from the original circle to the smaller circles. But don't stop there!

The ideas in the small circles can lead to yet more ideas, which you can write in even smaller circles. Eventually, you'll write an idea in a little circle out near one of the corners of your paper. That idea will click for you.

### Brainstorming

Have you ever sat down with a group and talked until you've come up with an idea for a project you are working on, whether it was to plan a trip or organize a party? Then you were *brainstorming*. As all of you kept talking, group members may have up come up with new ideas that

# WRITING IT RIGHT

## Model Idea Web

The following idea web models the ideas of a student who is narrowing down the general topic of "Animals."

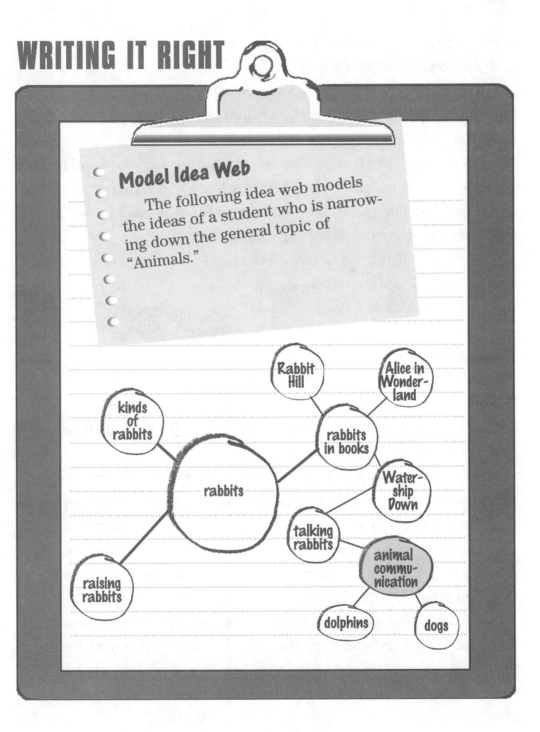

seemed silly or impractical, but one idea led to another, and you eventually hit on an idea that worked.

Brainstorming a topic for a research paper works the same way, except that you do it by yourself, and you use a pencil and paper. Start by writing down the first topic that comes into your head, then the second, the one after that, and so on. Try to free your mind and let the ideas come. Without worrying whether anyone will see what you write, add everything that comes to mind to your list. It doesn't matter if some of your ideas are completely ridiculous. There's an excellent chance that all the ideas that don't work will eventually lead to (at least!) one idea that does.

## Freewriting

If you've tried brainstorming, but your brain just isn't "storming" along, try a similar method called *freewriting*. Simply start writing down the thoughts that come to your mind, and then don't stop! Keep writing, no matter what! As one thought flows freely into another, you'll begin to make connections to ideas that interest you. Eventually, you may find yourself writing down several ideas that you find appealing. Review your freewriting and underline the ideas that interest you most. Write more about these ideas until you find your topic.

**INSIDE SECRET**

## Idea Webs versus Brainstorms

The main difference between an idea web and a brainstorm is that an idea web flows from one related topic to another. Although brainstorming includes a wide variety of ideas, they are not necessarily "connected" to one another.

# WRITING IT RIGHT

### Model Freewriting

Here are the thoughts of a student who used freewriting to arrive at a topic on animal communication.

Help! I can't think of a topic. Everything I can think of seems stupid, but I'll just write it down anyway. OK, here goes. I could write about, uh, rabbits! That's the first thing I thought of. Maybe because I just read that book about rabbits called <u>Watership Down</u>. The rabbits in the book could talk. Rabbit communication—I don't think I'll find much on that. But what about other animals? Forget that—animal communication is much too big a topic. What about dog communication? I am interested in dogs. I know my dog communicates in lots of ways. I'd like to know more about what she's trying to tell me. I think I've got my topic!

## Narrow Your Topic

Earlier, this chapter talked about avoiding topics that are too broad, such as "The American Revolution." Whether your teacher has given you a large general topic or you've decided on one yourself, you'll need a few strategies for narrowing a general topic down to a size that you can manage.

### Ask Questions

Begin by asking yourself questions about your general topic. For example, with the broad topic "Plants," you might ask:

- "How do plants grow?"

- "What do plants need?"

- "How do plants survive in the desert?"

- "What are some unusual kinds of plants?"

These questions could lead to topics such as "Plant Life in the Desert" or "Strange Plants—and How They Got That Way."

### Make a Pyramid Chart

If seeing your ideas organized on paper helps you think clearly, a *pyramid diagram* is a graphic organizer that can help you narrow a topic. Get a sheet of notebook paper, and in the center of the top line, write down your general topic. To continue with the same example, write "Plants" at the center of the top line. On the next line, beneath the general topic, write two topics that are smaller than the general topic; leave a small amount of space between each topic. You might write "Desert Plants" and "Rain Forest Plants."

On the third line, write two even smaller topics beneath each of the topics on the second line. Under "Desert Plants," you might write

"Cacti" and "Trees of the Desert." Beneath "Rain Forest Plants," you might write "Plants That Live in Trees" and "Plants of the Forest Floor." You can go on and on until you reach a topic that seems right. If you go too far, you might reach a topic that is too narrow. In that case, go up a line or two to find one that is just right.

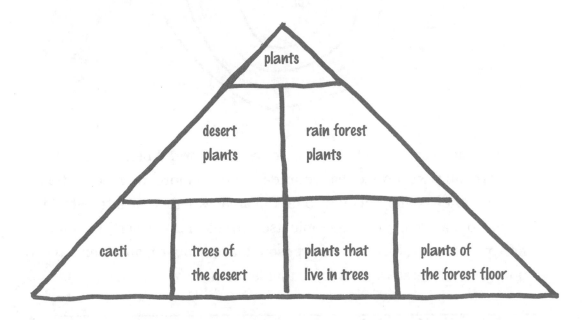

## Make a Target Diagram

You may prefer another type of graphic organizer—the *target diagram.* A target diagram is especially useful if you want to write down more than just two ideas for each preceding idea. It allows your thoughts to flow a little more freely, and gradually you can see the direction that interests you most.

Draw a circle in the center of a sheet of paper. Around that circle, draw several larger circles so that your blank diagram looks like a target. In the central circle, write your general topic. Then, in the outer circles, start writing narrower and narrower topics until you reach one that seems just narrow enough.

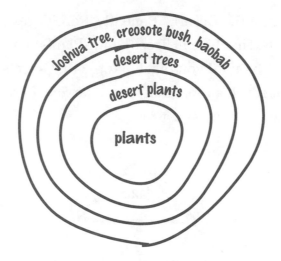

You may have to add outer circles as you work. When you finish, you probably will notice that your ideas moved more in one direction than another—a helpful clue about the areas where your interests lie. You also may go beyond the topic itself (trees of the desert) to some narrower topics (Joshua tree, creosote bush, baobab), and then have to pull back a level to avoid a topic that is too narrow.

## Schedule Your Work

Congratulations! If you've been following along with the models in this chapter, it's a good bet that you've succeeded in finding a good topic for your research paper. You are ready to move on to the next step: beginning your research. Take time to schedule your work, to make sure you finish your paper on time—without having to stay up late three nights in a row before the due date!

Start by making a copy of the sample Scheduling Form (Appendix A) at the back of this book. Then, write in the last thing first—**the due date.** Work backward from there, estimating the time you'll need for each task: researching and taking notes, making an outline, writing a first draft, revising your first draft, and preparing your final presentation. In order to make realistic estimates, consider which jobs will take the most time (research and writing a first draft, probably) and which will take the least (preparing your final presentation, probably).

Stick to your schedule as closely as possible. If you find yourself moving more slowly than you expected, keep revising your schedule as you work. Remember one important thing—**the date at the end doesn't change!**

Ready Set... REVIEW

## Practice Finding a Topic

1. Use a pyramid chart or a target diagram to narrow a general topic to a more manageable one. Start with a broad topic of your own choosing, or use one of the following:

   - animals
   - space
   - prehistoric times
   - music
   - holidays
   - transportation

2. Decide whether each of the following topics is too broad, too narrow, or just right for a term paper. If you are unsure, do a little research to find books or other material about the topic.

   - the history of the automobile
   - plants and animals of the Antarctic
   - European kings and queens
   - the amazing human heart
   - Egyptian hieroglyphic writing

# LOOK IT UP

✓ **Where to Begin**

✓ **Research Questions: The 5 Ws + H**

✓ **The Library Catalog**

✓ **The Periodical Index**

✓ **More Sources**

✓ **Source Cards**

*You did some early research to find a topic for your paper. Now it's time to revisit those sources to explore them some more.*

You've already done some early research, taking a quick look at an encyclopedia and the Internet. Although you won't take notes yet, these sources will help you gain important background information. This exploratory research tells you know where you're going and what to look for when you do your actual research—a topic we'll discuss in the next chapter.

## Where to Begin

To get a basic overview of information on any topic, start with the encyclopedia and the Internet. Many people have access to these sources right in their own homes, but they are also available at most libraries.

### Encyclopedias

Remember when you were a little kid? You may have depended entirely on encyclopedias when you wrote reports. Now that you're older, you'll mainly use other sources, but a good general encyclopedia—one that

WHAT A GREAT VIEW. IN FACT, IT'S AN OVERVIEW!

has information on all sorts of topics—is still an excellent place to begin your exploring. General encyclopedias don't delve deeply into most topics, but they give you that broad overview you need.

## Choosing an Encyclopedia

What makes a "good" encyclopedia? First of all, look for one that includes a separate book for each one or two letters of the alphabet. One-volume encyclopedias probably do not provide enough information on your topic. Next, you want to find an encyclopedia that is on your level. The ones written mainly for adult researchers may be too difficult or too technical for your purposes. Of course, you don't want to use an encyclopedia written for very young children, either. A few examples of multivolume encyclopedias that are written at an appropriate level for young adults are the *Encyclopedia Americana, World Book Encyclopedia, Britannica Junior Encyclopaedia,* and the online encyclopedia *Encarta.* Some encyclopedias in book form also come on CDs that you can use at the library or install on a personal computer.

If you're using encyclopedias in the library, you can find them in the reference area. But remember, none of the books in the reference room can be taken out, so plan enough time to use them in the library.

## Using an Encyclopedia

Finding information in an encyclopedia is easy, but there's more to it than just looking up one word. For example, if your topic is dog communication, begin by looking up the word "dog." In the article on dogs, you might not find any specific information on how dogs communicate, but you may find a related topic on dog training. At the end of the article on dog training, you may find a whole list of related articles in the encyclopedia. Decide which ones are worth looking up. Remember that you have two words in your topic—*dog* and *communication.* If you look up "Communication," you might not find information about "Dog Communication," but you might find "animal communication." It's worth a try.

In addition to general encyclopedias, an encyclopedia that focuses specifically on your topic may be available. In the library you might find a single book or even a set of books called *The Encyclopedia of Dogs*. If you do, don't look up "Dogs," of course. Go straight for that second word in your topic—"Communication." An article under "Communication" in *The Dog Encyclopedia* might offer other ideas to look up—"Training," for example, or "Barking."

## The Internet for Exploration

In addition to encyclopedias, you can use the Internet as an exploration tool. In fact, surfing the Net to explore a topic is quite similar to using an encyclopedia. Instead of looking up a word in a book, type keywords into a search engine, such as Google, Yahoo!, excite, or WebCrawler, to take you to a list of Web sites related to your topic.

Like using an encyclopedia, using the Internet involves more than you might think. For example, a good set of keywords to start with might be "dog communication." But if you're not finding as many good sites as you would like, you can try different keywords—"dog behavior" or "barking." You might even try typing in a question, such as "Why do dogs bark?" "Why do dogs wag their tails?" or "How do dogs communicate?"

Once you get a list of Web sites that sound interesting, decide which ones to go ahead and read. Notice that the list you get when you use a keyword includes a short description of each Web site. That description can give you a clue to how useful the information on the Web site is for your purposes. For example, a partial list of sites—or hits—for the keywords "dog communication" might look like this:

- Dog Communication: Listen to Your Dog. I have a personal example of how listening to my dog helped save me from making the worst mistake of my life.

- Dog-to-Dog Communication: Article by Dr. Andrew Dodsworth. Various parts of a dog's body are involved in communication.

- Why Dogs Bark: Dr. Elizabeth Ryan, leading animal behaviorist, explains what dogs mean when they bark.

At a glance, you can see that the first Web site, an unscientific description of one person's experience, is not as helpful as the second and third, which offer information from experts.

You may see many titles and descriptions of Web sites that sound interesting, but don't spend too much time reading now. Remember, your goal, for the present, is to explore your topic, so pick and choose materials that move you toward that goal. However, you might want to write down or bookmark some Web addresses or print out a few of the best articles for later use.

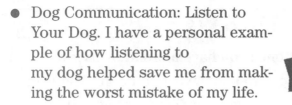

KEY 2

## Know Your Sources

Not all information on the Web is reliable. One way to judge a Web site is to look at its address. For example, an address ending in ".edu" means the site is connected to a college, university, or other school. (The letters *edu* stand for "education.") Such addresses often contain good information, but not always. Of course, useful sources can end in ".gov," ".com," or something else. If you have doubts about the accuracy of a site or want help finding more reliable sources, consult your librarian, teacher, or parent.

## Research Questions: The 5 Ws + H

This may sound strange, but once you have a broad overview of your topic, you know enough to know what you don't know. In other words, you know enough to ask questions—an important step in writing a research paper. Having specific questions (called "research questions") to answer as you continue your research helps you find the sources that are most helpful to you. Your questions also help you focus on what information you want your paper to contain and how to organize that information.

Have you ever heard of the 5 Ws + H? The 5 Ws stand for "What?" "Where?" "When?" "Why?" and "Who?" The H stands for "How?" Let the 5 Ws + H guide you in developing your list of research questions. One way to do this is to make a six-column chart with these headings: "What?" "Where?" "When?" "Why?" "Who?" and "How?" Try to write at least one question about your topic in each column, but don't worry if you have to leave one or more columns blank. The columns you fill in depend on your topic. For example, for "Dog Communication," you may not have questions in the "Where?" or "Who?" columns. Consider the questions you might come up with in the "What?" "When?" "Why?" and "How? columns:

| What? | Where? | When? | Why? | Who? | How? |
|-------|--------|-------|------|------|------|
| In what different ways do dogs communicate? | | | Why do dogs bark? Why do dogs growl? Why do dogs wag their tails? Why do dogs lick people's faces? | | How do dogs use sounds to communicate? How do dogs use "body language" to communicate? Do dogs use facial expressions to communicate (smile and frown)? |

Your own questions can guide your research by showing you what kind of information you need. You also can see how your research questions give you an idea of how your report might take shape. The questions in the chart could lead to a report that has two or three main parts—how dogs communicate with sounds, how dogs communicate with body language, and how dogs use facial expressions to communicate. Or the questions could lead to a report that concentrates on explaining several specific types of behavior.

Your next stop is the library. Be sure to take your questions along to remind yourself of the information you seek. And take two other things along—something to write with and a package of 3" × 5" index cards. Later in this chapter you'll learn what to do with them.

## The Library Catalog

An important part of your exploratory research is identifying the specific sources to use when you begin taking notes for your paper. The best place to start is the library catalog, which includes a list of all the books in your library. Assuming the catalog is online and you need help using it, ask the librarian to show you how. (Check to see if you can access your library catalog on your home computer too.)

You can search the library catalog in three ways—by subject, title, or author. A subject search shows the titles of books on your topic. To do a subject search, type in your topic. Then click on "subject." You will get a list of all the books in the library on your topic, including the title, author, and call number for each book. The call number is important because the books are placed on the shelves in numerical order according to call number.

If you happen to know particular authors or titles of books that you might want to use, do an author or title search. Type in the author's name to get a list of books by that author, or type in the title of a book to get information about that book.

In most online catalogs, you can get more information about a book by highlighting the title and clicking on "more information," "expanded view," or a similar phrase that appears on the screen. Then the catalog shows the name of the publisher, the place and date the book was published, whether or not the book is available, the call number, and where in the library it is located—the reference section, the adult nonfiction section, or the children's section. You also may be able to click on helpful options such as "More by this author" or "More titles like this."

## The Periodical Index

A periodical is a magazine. It's called a periodical because it is published *periodically*—every week or every month, for example. You can find a lot of useful information in periodicals. Information in periodicals is often more up-to-date than what you find in many books. For example, you may be using books that were published many years ago or even within the past year, but you may find a useful article in a magazine that was written just a few weeks ago. To locate articles on your topic, do a subject search in a printed index called the *Readers' Guide to Periodical Literature*. Your librarian can show you where to find it and how to use it. He or she also can help you find the actual periodicals and articles you decide to use.

## More Sources

In addition to books and periodicals, other sources can add up-to-the-minute information to your research, including news-

paper articles, articles on the Internet, and a variety of nonprint sources. We've discussed how to do an Internet search and how to judge the reliability of a Web site. You can also use the Internet to find newspaper articles. Most big-city newspapers have Web sites that offer an indexed list of all the articles they have published for years. To get to major newspaper Web sites, type in the name of the newspaper— *The New York Times*, for example—instead of a keyword. Follow the instructions on the site for accessing the newspaper's archives, which are a collection of articles from past issues.

## TV and Radio

Check television and radio listings for programs about your topic. Educational stations, such as the Public Broadcasting Service (PBS) and National Public Radio (NPR), are your best bet. If you listen to some programs as part of your research, make a note of the name of the program, the station, and the date and time of the broadcast.

## Personal Interviews

Perhaps you know someone who is an expert on your topic. Still supposing your topic is "Dog Communication," your vet or your dog's obedience-school teacher may very well be an expert. Information you learn from personal interviews with these people can add interest to your research paper and make it more lively.

To set up an interview, explain to your expert that you are writing a research paper, describe the topic, and politely ask the person if he or she would be willing to spend a specific amount of time—half an hour, perhaps—talking to you. Ask your expert what place, date, and time is convenient for him or her. Be on time for the interview, and dress neatly to show you appreciate that this person is taking time to meet with you. Bring a pencil and paper for taking notes. If you want to tape-record the interview, ask permission first (because some people do not want to be taped). Most important, prepare a list of questions in advance.

If you plan to do an interview, save it for last. Before you've completed your research, you may not know what questions to ask. When you have all the information you can find from print and nonprint sources, you can use the interview to answer questions you still have. You also can ask your expert to express an opinion about information you've found in other sources. But do think about the interview and set it up now, so everyone has time to look at his or her calendar and set aside time in advance.

## Source Cards

Earlier in this chapter, we mentioned taking a pack of 3" × 5" index cards to the library. Here's why. As you search the library catalog, the *Readers' Guide,* and any other indexes you may use, you'll want to keep careful records for every source you find. These records help you find your sources when you're ready to use them. And you'll need them when the time comes to provide complete information about your sources at the end of your paper.

To keep good records, be sure to fill in the following information for every source card. (You can look at the sample source cards we've provided to find an example of each part.)

### Source Number

Assign a number to each source, and write this number in the upper left corner of the source card. Later, when you take notes from your sources, you can use these numbers to show where each piece of information came from. Using numbers is more efficient than writing the titles of books over and over again. This also helps because, in your final paper, you need to match numbers to names when crediting the source of your facts and ideas.

## Call Number

A call number is a description of the place where the source is located. If your source card is for a nonfiction book in the library, write its call number in the upper right corner. If the card is for another type of source, write where you found that information so that you are able to locate the source again.

## Information About the Source

In the center of the card, write the name of the author and the title of the source. For a book, include the place of publication, the publisher, and the publication or copyright date. For a magazine, include the name of the magazine, the date of the issue, and the page numbers of the article. On the sample cards below, notice how we've punctuated this information. This shows the standard punctuation that your teacher probably wants you to use when you list your sources at the end of your paper.

When you complete your source cards, stack them in order of their source number. Then put a rubber band around them or keep them in a small file envelope or box, and carry them with you to the library or anywhere else you plan to continue your research.

The index cards help you keep track of important records. During your exploratory research, fill in one card for each source you discover. These source cards are important: If you fill them in exactly the way we show you in the following examples, you'll have all the necessary information at your fingertips.

# WRITING IT RIGHT

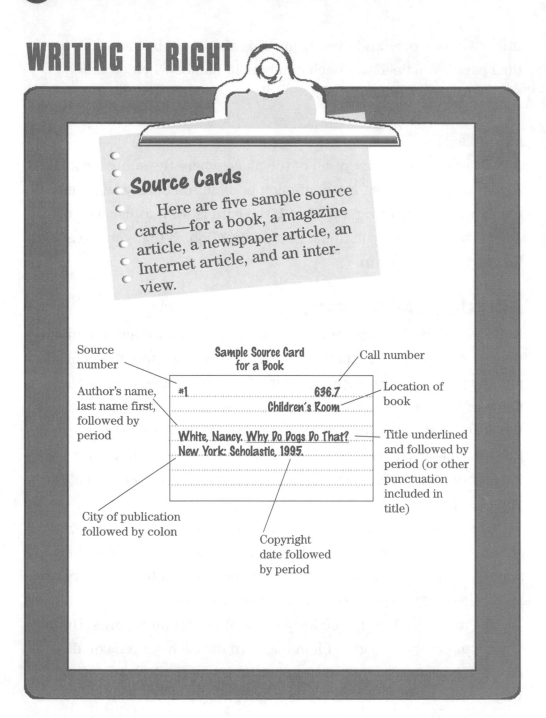

## Source Cards

Here are five sample source cards—for a book, a magazine article, a newspaper article, an Internet article, and an interview.

Source number

Author's name, last name first, followed by period

**Sample Source Card for a Book**

```
#1                        636.7
              Children's Room

White, Nancy. Why Do Dogs Do That?
New York: Scholastic, 1995.
```

Call number

Location of book

Title underlined and followed by period (or other punctuation included in title)

City of publication followed by colon

Copyright date followed by period

# WRITING IT RIGHT

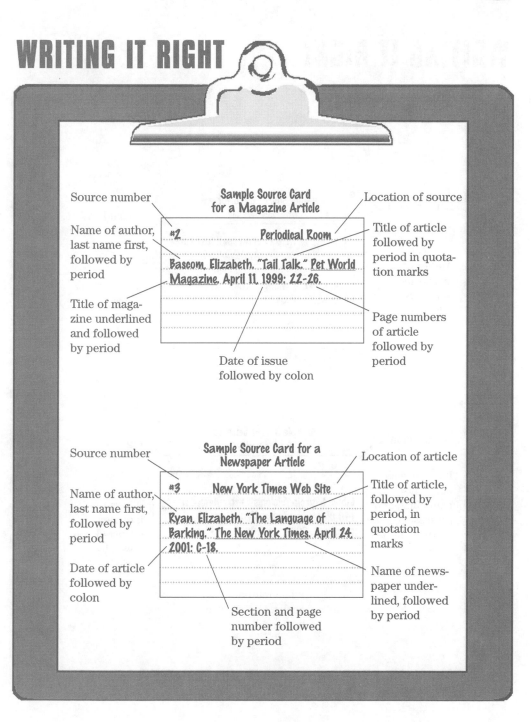

**Sample Source Card for a Magazine Article**

Source number

Name of author, last name first, followed by period

Title of magazine underlined and followed by period

Location of source

Title of article followed by period in quotation marks

#2                    Periodical Room

Bascom, Elizabeth. "Tail Talk." Pet World Magazine. April 11, 1999: 22-26.

Page numbers of article followed by period

Date of issue followed by colon

**Sample Source Card for a Newspaper Article**

Source number

Name of author, last name first, followed by period

Date of article followed by colon

Location of article

Title of article, followed by period, in quotation marks

#3        New York Times Web Site

Ryan, Elizabeth. "The Language of Barking." The New York Times. April 24, 2001: C-18.

Name of newspaper underlined, followed by period

Section and page number followed by period

# WRITING IT RIGHT

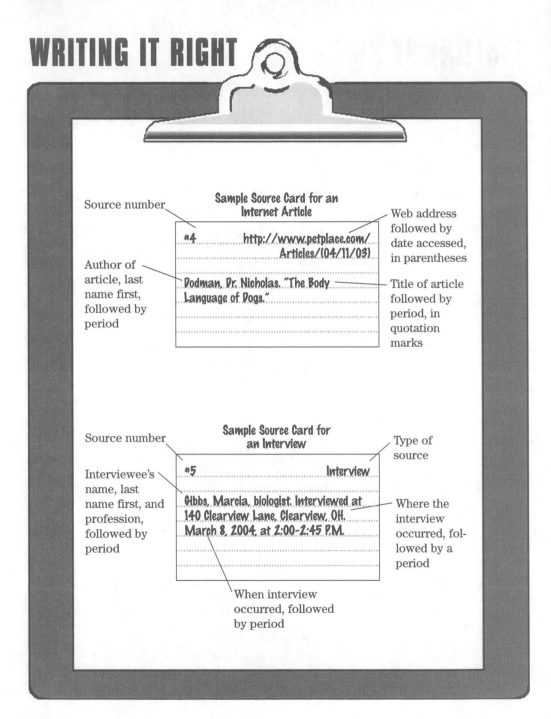

**Sample Source Card for an Internet Article**

Source number

#4          http://www.petplace.com/ Articles/(04/11/03)

Web address followed by date accessed, in parentheses

Author of article, last name first, followed by period

Dodman, Dr. Nicholas. "The Body Language of Dogs."

Title of article followed by period, in quotation marks

**Sample Source Card for an Interview**

Source number

#5                    Interview

Type of source

Interviewee's name, last name first, and profession, followed by period

Gibbs, Marcia, biologist. Interviewed at 140 Clearview Lane, Clearview, OH, March 8, 2004, at 2:00-2:45 P.M.

Where the interview occurred, followed by a period

When interview occurred, followed by period

## Ready, Set, REVIEW

### Practice Looking It Up

1. Write source cards for the following:

- A book called *Dogwatching* by Desmond Morris, published by Crown Publishers in New York in 1987. The call number in the library catalog is 636.7, and the book is found in the adult section of the library.
- A magazine article called "Conversations with My Dog," from a magazine called *Dog's Life*. The article was published on June 8, 2000, and appeared on pages 12–14 of the magazine. The magazine can be found in your library in the periodical room.
- An interview you plan to conduct with Dr. Wilma Mendel on August 10 of this year. You plan to meet Dr. Mendel at her office at 300 Central Avenue in Clearview, Ohio, at 3:30 P.M.

2. Using a computer search engine, such as Yahoo!, Google, or excite, find two Web sites that provide information on each of the following topics:

- "The League of Nations"
- "Pasteurization"
- "The Tennessee Valley Authority (TVA)"

KEY 2

# TAKE NOTES

✓ **Use Sources Efficiently**

✓ **Methods for Note Taking**

✓ **Effective Note Taking**

✓ **Organize Your Notes**

*Preliminary research and exploratory research— that's all done now. Get ready for what you might call your "real" research.*

Now you can get your hands on the sources you identified and take notes on the information. And because you're prepared for this, you can expect the process to go smoothly.

Your first step is to locate your sources and get yourself settled—either at a table in the library, or at home if you're using sources that you can take home. Be sure to have your source cards and research questions with you. Other supplies you'll need depend on the note-taking method you choose.

## Use Sources Efficiently

Most articles and some of the books you use, especially those from the children's room at the library, are probably short enough that you can read them from beginning to end in a reasonable amount of time. Others, however, may be too long for you to do that, and some are likely to cover much more than just your topic. Use the table of contents and the index in a longer book to find the parts of the book that contain information on your topic. When you turn to those parts, skim them to make sure they contain information you can use. Feel free to skip parts that don't relate to your questions, so you can get the information you need as quickly and efficiently as possible.

## Methods for Note Taking

WARNING: Do not—repeat, do not—start reading a book and writing down information on a sheet of notebook paper. If you make this mistake, you'll end up with a lot of disorganized scribbling that may be practically useless when you're ready to outline your paper and write a first draft. Some students who tried this had to cut up their notes into tiny strips, spread them out on the floor, and then tape the strips back together in order to put their information in an order that made sense. Other students couldn't even do that—without going to a photocopier first—because they had written on both sides of the paper. To avoid that kind of trouble, use the tried-and-true method students have been using for years—take notes on index cards.

### Taking Notes on Index Cards

As you begin reading your sources, use either 3" × 5" or 4" × 6" index cards to write down information you might use in your paper. The first thing to remember is: Write only one idea on each card. Even if you

write only a few words on one card, don't write anything about a new idea on that card. Begin a new card instead. Also, keep all your notes for one card only on that card. It's fine to write on both the front and back of a card, but don't carry the same note over to a second card. If you have that much to write, you probably have more than one idea.

After you complete a note card, write the source number of the book you used in the upper left corner of the card. Below the source number, write the exact number or numbers of the pages on which you found the information. In the upper right corner, write one or two words that describe the specific subject of the card. These words are like a headline that describes the main information on the card. Be as clear as possible because you will need these headlines later.

After you finish taking notes from a source, write a check mark on your source card as a reminder that you've gone through that source thoroughly and written down all the important information you found there. That way, you won't wonder later whether you should go back and read that source again.

## Taking Notes on Your Computer

Another way to take notes is on your computer. In order to use this method, you have to rely completely on sources that you can take home, unless you have a laptop computer that you can take with you to the library.

If you do choose to take notes on your computer, think of each entry on your screen as one in a pack of electronic note cards. Write your notes exactly as if you were using index cards. Be sure to leave space between each note so that they don't run together and look confusing when you're ready to use them. You might want to insert a page break between each "note card."

When deciding whether to use note cards or a computer, remember one thing—high-tech is not always better. Many students find low-tech index cards easier to organize and use than computer notes that have to be moved around by cutting and pasting. In the end, you're the one who knows best how you work, so the choice is up to you.

# WRITING IT RIGHT

## Model Note Cards
### Two Sample Note Cards from the Same Source

Suppose you start reading your first source—*Why Do Dogs Do That?* by Nancy White. You don't see any information that you think is important for your paper until you come to the following passage on page 10:

*When a dog barks at home, he is usually telling his human family, "Someone's coming!"*

| #1 | Barking |
|---|---|
| p. 10 | |
| Barking at home can mean "Someone's coming!" | |

You continue reading and find this passage on page 11:

*A wagging tail can mean different things: "Hi! I'm glad to see you!" "Hi! Want to play?"*

This is good stuff too. You should definitely make a note—but not on the same card. Start a second card.

| #1 | Tail wagging |
|---|---|
| p. 11 | |
| Tail wagging can mean dog is happy to see you or wants to play. | |

KEY 3

## Effective Note Taking

Knowing the best format for notes is important, but knowing what to write on your cards or on your computer is essential. Strong notes are the backbone of a good research paper.

### Not Too Much or Too Little

When researching, you're likely to find a lot of interesting information that you never knew before. That's great! You can never learn too much. But for now your goal is to find information you can use in your paper. Giving in to the temptation to take notes on every detail you find in your research can lead to a huge volume of notes—many of which you won't use at all. This can become difficult to manage at later stages, so limit yourself to information that really belongs in your paper. If you think a piece of information might be useful but you aren't sure, ask yourself whether it helps answer one of your research questions.

Writing too much is one pitfall; writing too little is another. Consider this scenario: You've been working in the library for a couple of hours, and your hand grows tired from writing. You come to a fairly complicated passage about how to tell if a dog is angry,

## Shorthand

One way to save time when taking notes is called "shorthand." It's a way of writing that uses symbols to avoid writing out every word completely. Here are some standard shorthand words and their meanings:

w/ = with
w/o = without
wh/ = which
+ = and; also
esp = especially
∴ = therefore

so you say to yourself, "I don't have to write all this down. I'll remember." But you won't remember—especially after all the reading and note taking you have been doing. If you find information you know you want to use later on, get it down. If you're too tired, take a break or take off the rest of the day and return tomorrow when you're fresh.

## To Note or Not to Note

What if you come across an idea or piece of information that you've already found in another source? Should you write it down again? You don't want to end up with a whole stack of cards with the same information on each one. On the other hand, knowing that more than one source agrees on a particular point is helpful. Here's the solution: Simply add the number of the new source to the note card that already has the same piece of information written on it.

What if you come across an idea or piece of information that contradicts something you've found in another source? Suppose you read in one source that dogs wag their tails to show they are happy, but another source says that tail wagging doesn't always mean a dog is happy: It could even mean the dog wants to fight. How can you decide which source is right? For now, take notes on both sources. In your paper, you may want to come right out and say that sources disagree on this point. You may even want to support one opinion or the other— if you think you have a strong enough argument based on facts from your research.

## Paraphrasing—Not Copying

Have you ever heard the word *plagiarism*? It means copying someone else's words and claiming them as your own. It's really a kind of stealing, and there are strict rules against it.

KEY 3

The trouble is many students plagiarize without meaning to do so. The problem starts at the note-taking stage. As a student takes notes, he or she may simply copy the exact words from a source. The student doesn't put quotation marks around the words to show that they are someone else's. When it comes time to draft the paper, the student doesn't even remember that those words were copied from a source, and the words find their way into the draft and then into the final paper. Without intending to do so, that student has plagiarized, or stolen, another person's words.

The way to avoid plagiarism is to *paraphrase*, or write down ideas in your own words rather than copy them exactly. Look again at the model note cards in this chapter, and notice that the words in the notes are not the same as the words from the sources. Some of the notes are not even written in complete sentences. Writing in incomplete sentences is one way to make sure you don't copy—and it saves you time, energy, and space. When you write a draft of your paper, of course, you will use complete sentences.

## To Quote or Not to Quote

In some instances, copying words from a source is OK—but only when you put quotation marks around the words and tell, in your paper, who said them. Then you are giving credit to the real writer.

Quoting from a source—if you credit the author—is perfectly permissible, but avoid doing it often. Use a quotation only if an author has said something so well that whoever reads your paper benefits from knowing the author's exact words.

The following two examples from *Why Do Dogs Do That?* show when to quote and when not to:

> A dog's brain isn't made for learning words, and a dog's mouth isn't made for talking. So dogs won't ever learn to talk.

When you take notes on that passage, paraphrase it. Nothing here is so special that you need to quote it. Your notes might look like this:

> Dogs can't talk—brain and mouth not right for speech.

You might want to quote the passage below, however, because the author makes her point in a "catchy" way.

> Dogs make great friends. But when it comes to conversation, forget it!

If you want to quote that passage, copy it word-for-word in your notes; then place quotation marks around it. Be sure you've copied everything exactly as it is, including any punctuation. In your paper, the passage might end up like this:

> As Nancy White says in her book *Why Do Dogs Do That?*, "Dogs make great friends. But when it comes to conversation, forget it!"

Even the best quotations lose their effect if you use too many of them. If your paper contains one quotation after another, your readers may wonder where to find the part that you wrote yourself.

## Organize Your Notes

Once you've used all your sources and taken all your notes, what do you have? You have a stack of cards (or if you've taken notes on a computer, screen after screen of entries) about a lot of stuff in no particular order. Now you need to organize your notes in order to turn them into the powerful tool that helps you outline and draft your paper. Following are some ideas on how to do this, so get your thinking skills in gear to start doing the job for your own paper.

## Organizing Note Cards

The beauty of using index cards to take notes is that you can move them around until they are in the order you want. You don't have to go through complicated cutting-and-pasting procedures, as you would on your computer, and you can lay your cards out where you can see them all at once. One word of caution—work on a surface where your cards won't fall on the floor while you're organizing them.

Start by sorting all your cards with the same headlines into the same piles, since all of these note cards are about the same basic idea. (You don't have to worry about keeping notes from the same sources together because each card is marked with a number identifying its source.)

Next, arrange the piles of cards so that the order the ideas appear in makes sense. Experts have named six basic types of order. One—or a combination of these—may work for you.

- *Chronological, or Time, Order* covers events in the order in which they happened. This kind of order works best for papers that discuss historical events or tell about a person's life.

- *Spatial Order* organizes your information by its place or position. This kind of order can work for papers about geography or about how to design something—a garden, for example.

- *Cause and Effect* discusses how one event or action leads to another. This kind of organization works well if your paper explains a scientific process or events in history.

- *Problem/Solution* explains a problem and one or more ways in which it can be solved. You might use this type of organization for a paper about an environmental issue, such as global warming.

- *Compare and Contrast* discusses similarities and differences between people, things, events, or ideas.

- *Order of Importance* explains an idea, starting with its most important aspects first and ending with the least important aspects—or the other way around.

Suppose your card piles have the following headlines: "barking," "tail wagging," "face licking," "rolling over," "growling," "showing teeth." How will you arrange them? Here's one way your thinking might go:

> My cards are sorted by different types of behavior. I know that each of these behaviors communicates something different. So I could use a compare-and-contrast organization. I could start with sounds dogs make and move on to facial expression and then body language. I'll go from one end of the dog's body to the other—ears to tail—and end up with whole-body language. So I'd be combining two kinds of order—compare-and-contrast and spatial.

After you determine your basic organization, arrange your piles accordingly. You'll end up with three main piles—one for sounds, one for facial expressions, and one for body language. Go through each pile and put the individual cards in an order that makes sense. Don't forget that you can move your cards around, trying out different organizations, until you are satisfied that one idea flows logically into another. Use a paper clip or rubber band to hold the piles together, and then stack them in the order you choose. Put a big rubber band around the whole stack so the cards stay in order.

## Organizing Notes on a Computer

If you've taken notes on a computer, organize them in much the same way you would organize index cards. The difference is that you use the cut-and-paste functions on your computer rather than moving cards around. The advantage is that you end up with something that's already typed—something you can eventually turn into an outline without having to copy anything over. The disadvantage is that you may have more trouble moving computer notes around than note cards: You can't lay your notes out and look at them all at once, and you may get confused when trying to find where information has moved within a long file on your computer screen.

**KEY 3**

## Ready Set... REVIEW

### Practice Taking Notes

1. Suppose that you are writing a social studies paper about knights during the Middle Ages in Europe. The passage below is from a book that you have labeled source #4. Make three note cards based on the passage.

When a nobleman became a professional soldier, he was called a knight. Knights followed special rules of behavior. These rules, which were called *chivalry*, required that a knight be brave, treat his enemies fairly and respectfully, be honest, and be loyal. He also had to be polite to women.

For protection in battle, a knight wore a heavy metal helmet and suit of armor and carried a shield. He also carried a sword and other weapons such as a *lance*, or long pole.

2. For each of the following topics, decide which type of organization might be most useful when arranging your notes: chronological, order of importance, spatial, cause and effect, problem/solution, compare and contrast. You might choose more than one type for a topic.

- What led the American colonies to declare independence from Britain
- The planets of our solar system
- The polio epidemic of the 1950s, and how it was controlled

# OUTLINE YOUR PAPER

✓ **What Is an Outline?**

✓ **From Notes to Outline**

✓ **Rules for Outlining**

✓ **Planning Your Beginning and Ending**

*Your research paper is beginning to take shape. The next step is to turn those piles of note cards into an outline.*

With a good outline, you are better able to write a logical, well-organized paper. You may even start to feel as if your paper can practically write itself!

## What Is an Outline?

An outline is sort of a list of all the ideas that you will discuss in the body of your paper. It's more than just a list, though. It's a list that is arranged in a special way so that the bigger, main ideas stand out from the supporting details (the facts or examples that support the main ideas).

In traditional outline form, the biggest ideas, or main topics, are numbered with Roman numerals. The second biggest ideas, or subtopics, are indented and use capital letters. Supporting ideas, or details, are indented farther and numbered with Arabic numerals. Here's an example:

    I.  First Main Topic
        A.  Subtopic
            1.  Detail
            2.  Detail
        B.  Subtopic
            1.  Detail
            2.  Detail
            3.  Detail
        C.  Subtopic
            1.  Detail
            2.  Detail
    II. Second Main Topic
        A.  Subtopic
            1.  Detail
            2.  Detail

Some outlines include even more levels of detail, which are even farther indented, using lowercase letters. You probably won't be including such small details in your outline, but here's an example of how it would look if you wanted to include them:

    2. Detail
        a. Smaller detail
        b. Smaller detail
        c. Smaller detail

## From Notes to Outline

The way you organized your index cards gives you a good idea of how to organize your outline. Remember how you sorted your note cards by headline and then made bigger piles of cards? In the example, the note cards were sorted by headline into different types of dog behavior—barking, face-licking, growling, and so on. Then the cards were organized into three bigger piles—sounds, facial expressions, and body language. Now those three big piles become the main topics in the outline—Roman numerals I, II, and III. The headlines become the subtopics, which are labeled with capital letters. The information in your notes contains your details, which are labeled with Arabic numbers.

Your computer's word processing program probably has an outlining feature. If you want to use it, go to the index under the "Help" function in your word processing program. Type in "outlining," and then follow the instructions that appear on your screen.

KEY 4

# WRITING IT RIGHT

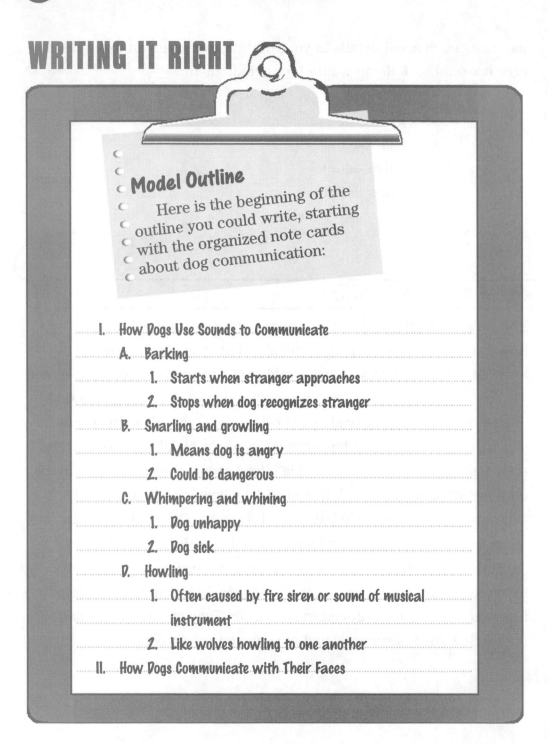

### Model Outline

Here is the beginning of the outline you could write, starting with the organized note cards about dog communication:

I.   How Dogs Use Sounds to Communicate
   A.   Barking
      1.   Starts when stranger approaches
      2.   Stops when dog recognizes stranger
   B.   Snarling and growling
      1.   Means dog is angry
      2.   Could be dangerous
   C.   Whimpering and whining
      1.   Dog unhappy
      2.   Dog sick
   D.   Howling
      1.   Often caused by fire siren or sound of musical instrument
      2.   Like wolves howling to one another
II.   How Dogs Communicate with Their Faces

## Rules for Outlining

The model outline follows certain rules. The following rules can
help you write an outline that leads to a well-organized paper:

1. Use Roman numerals to indicate main topics.
2. Use capital letters to indicate subtopics.
3. Use Arabic numbers to indicate details.
4. Include at least two main topics. (Our example has three.)
5. Include least two entries at each level. In other words, have at least two main topics. Under each main topic, include at least two subtopics. And under each subtopic, have at least two details.

Why do these rules matter? They matter because when you draft your paper, the main topics become paragraphs, and the subtopics become sentences. You need more than one paragraph to make a paper, you need more than one sentence to make a paragraph, and you need more than one detail to support an idea.

INSIDE SECRET

### Use Fragments

Even though you've been taught not to use sentence fragments, here's one exception. When writing your outline, don't use complete sentences. It will be faster this way, and you won't be tempted to copy sentences you wrote in haste into your paper.

KEY 4

## Planning Your Beginning and Ending

Now that you've completed your outline, it's time to think about how your paper will begin and end. You don't have to have the final wording down, but having a plan will help you enormously when you begin your actual writing. Knowing how your paper will begin and end will make the middle easier to write by giving you a "frame" to work within.

### Your Thesis Statement

Every paper should begin with a very important sentence or group of sentences that tell the reader—right up front—the main idea of the

paper. That's right—the one big, main idea of the whole paper. The technical term for this part of a paper is the *thesis statement*.

You've probably had the main idea for your paper in your head since you chose your topic. Now, by looking over your outline, you should be able to put that idea into one or two clearly worded sentences. Look at your main topics—the ones with Roman numerals in front of them. (In our example, they are "How Dogs Use Sounds to Communicate" and "How Dogs Communicate with Their Faces.") Ask yourself these questions about your main topics:

- What do these ideas add up to?

- How are these main ideas related to one another?

- What's an even bigger idea that covers all of them?

By asking—and answering—these questions, you can come up with a thesis statement. For our example, it's something like, "Dogs use sounds, their faces, and their bodies to communicate with other dogs and with humans." Now you've got your thesis statement. When you write your first draft, try to present that statement in the most interesting and inviting way possible.

## Your Conclusion

Here's how one teacher tells her students how to write a paper in three simple steps:

1. Tell your readers what you're going to say.
2. Say it.
3. Tell them what you said.

You've already planned how to tell your readers what you're going to say. That's your thesis statement. You know what you'll say. That's the main part of your paper, which you've already outlined. In your conclusion, you'll tell your readers what you said—and maybe a little more.

In your conclusion you sum up, or review, your main points. If you want to make your paper even better, try helping your readers answer the question "So what?" In other words, tell them what they can do with the information you've given them, or tell them why the points you made are particularly interesting or important. You might even end with a question that will keep readers thinking about your paper after they've finished reading it.

For a conclusion to the dog communication paper, you might write, "Dogs communicate a wide range of feelings, from fear to friendliness, by using sounds, facial expressions, and body language." That pretty much sums up your paper. In answer to the "So What?" question, you might add, "Knowing about dog communication can be very useful." Then you'll need a few examples to prove how useful it can be to understand dogs. If you want to leave readers with a question, you might write something like, "Look and listen to the next dog you meet. What is the dog trying to say?"

If you think now about your thesis statement and your conclusion, you'll have your whole paper planned. Writing your first draft can be a piece of cake.

*Ready Set*

# REVIEW

## Practice Outlining

1. Suppose you are writing a paper about the Vikings. You've taken notes on index cards and divided them into three main piles—cards about the Vikings' way of life, the Vikings' ships, and the Vikings' discoveries. In the pile of cards that are about the Vikings' ships, some of the cards have the headline "How ships were made" and some have the headline "What the ships looked like." Here are the five cards in that pile:

> #1          How ships were made
> p. 10
>
> Made of wood

> #3          How ships were made
> p. 36
>
> Wooden planks overlapped like the side of a wooden house.

> #4        What the ships looked like
> p. 18
>
> Some about 78 feet long and more than 16 feet wide

*(Continued)*

KEY 4

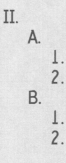

> #4          What the ships looked like
> p. 20
>
> Square sail on mast about 40 feet
> high.

> #5          What the ships looked like
> p. 18
>
> Had carving of dragon on front to
> frighten enemies

Now copy the following outline form, and fill it in with information from the cards.

II.
   A.
      1.
      2.
   B.
      1.
      2.

2. The following notes could be from research on the American Revolutionary War. Here, they are in no particular order. Organize them as they might appear in an outline for a term paper, arranging them as main topics, subtopics, and details:

- Parliament's 1765 Stamp Act forced colonists to pay taxes on many products; colonists resented being taxed when they had no representation in Parliament.

- In July 1776, the Continental Congress adopted the Declaration of Independence, which declared the United States a free nation.

- The Sugar Act of 1763 put a tax on sugar and molasses.

- Relations between Britain and the American colonies grew worse beginning in the early 1760s, with the passage of a series of unpopular laws that imposed new taxes on the colonists.

- Fighting broke out between the colonies and Britain in 1775.

- The Sugar Act placed a three-penny tax on every gallon of molasses sold in the colonies; molasses was a much-used product.

- The Tea Act, passed in 1773, placed a tax on tea; the resentment of colonists led to the famous Boston Tea Party, when colonists disguised as Native Americans dumped a cargo of tea into Boston Harbor.

- The colonists' anger over the Sugar Act led to a reduction in the tax on molasses from three cents to one cent per gallon, but their anger did not go away.

- Colonial Minutemen fought soldiers of the British army at Lexington and Concord, Massachusetts, in 1775, resulting in several dead and wounded on both sides.

- The series of taxes imposed on the colonies gradually led a large number of colonists to believe that they could no longer live under the British government.

- The first major battle of the Revolution, Bunker Hill, was fought in the Boston area in 1776 and resulted in many casualties.

KEY 4

# KEY 5

## CREATE YOUR FIRST DRAFT

✓ **Follow a Format**

✓ **Start Writing**

✓ **Cite Your Sources**

✓ **Choose a Title**

FIRST DRAFT

*At last, you're ready to prepare your first draft. That means putting words down on paper—and more.*

efore you begin, you have some decisions to make about format, or how your paper will look. As you write, you have to think about presenting your ideas in a way that makes sense and holds your readers' interest. After you've completed your draft, make sure you've cited your sources completely and correctly. And the last thing you'll need to do is decide on the very first thing readers see—the title.

## Follow a Format

Many teachers tell their students exactly how their papers should
be formatted—for example, how wide the margins should be,
where and how the sources should be listed, and so on. If your teacher
has specified a format, be sure you have a list of the rules she or he has
established—and follow them! If not, you need to decide on questions
of format for yourself. Here are the main questions to consider:

- Should your report be written by hand or typed in a word
  processing program?

- If you are handwriting, should you write on every line or every
  other line?

- If you are handwriting, should you use both sides or only one
  side of the paper?

- If you are typing, should you use single space or double space?
  For typing, double spacing is standard.

- If you are using a computer, what type style (font) and size
  should you use? (Twelve-point Times or Times New Roman is
  standard.)

- What size should the margins be? Margins of 1" or 1.25" on each
  side are standard.

- How long should your report be—how many pages or words?

- Should you include illustrations? Are illustrations optional?

- How should you position your heading (and should it include
  information other than name, class, and date)?

- Should you include a separate title page?

- Should your bibliography (a list of your sources) appear on a
  separate page at the end of your report? That is standard.

- Should your bibliography list your sources in alphabetical order by last name of author? That is standard.

- Where should your page numbers appear? The standard position for page numbering is the upper right corner of each page.

If you are using a computer, choose and set up your margin widths, type size and style, and spacing now.

## Start Writing

Remember when we said that with a good outline you may feel as if your paper can practically write itself? If you follow your outline now, you can find out just how true that is. A paper has three main parts—the introduction (which contains your thesis statement),

I guess I wrote a great outline!

KEY 5

the body, and the conclusion. When you outlined your paper, you did the body first. Then you planned your thesis statement and your conclusion. For writing the first draft, let's begin at the beginning—with the introduction.

## Draft Your Introduction

Beginning your paper with an introductory paragraph serves two purposes. It grabs your readers' attention, and it contains your thesis statement—the main idea of your entire paper. When you wrote your outline, you drafted a rough thesis statement. Now build it into a paragraph that makes your readers want to know what you have to say. How you do that depends on your topic, but here are some general suggestions that may help:

- Relate your topic to your readers' own experiences. For example:

  Do you know anyone who is strong, brave, loyal, honest, fair, and always has good manners? Meet a knight from the Middle Ages.

- Begin with a fascinating or surprising fact. For example:

  If you thought Columbus was the first European explorer to cross the Atlantic Ocean, think again. Long before Columbus's voyages to the New World, bold explorers from the north were sailing the seas.

- Let readers know they are going to learn information they will find useful. For example:

  If you are interested in a career in space exploration, you can start preparing now.

Any of these approaches can help you get your paper off to a good start—with your readers on board!

# WRITING IT RIGHT

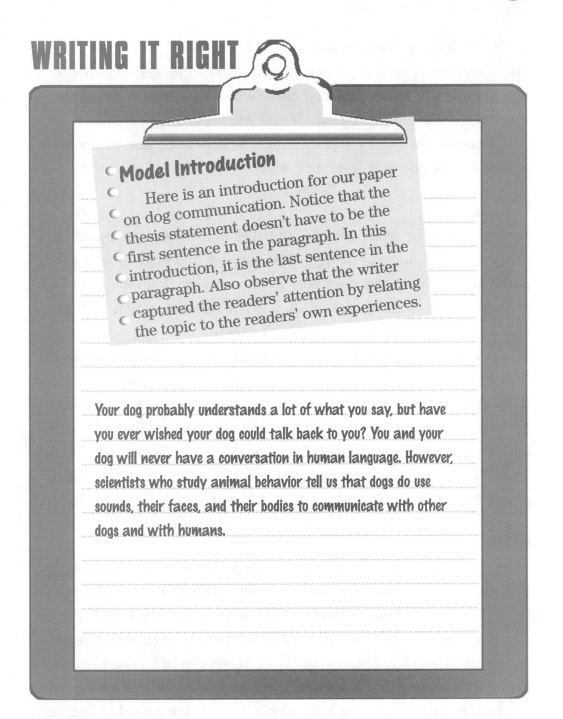

## Model Introduction

Here is an introduction for our paper on dog communication. Notice that the thesis statement doesn't have to be the first sentence in the paragraph. In this introduction, it is the last sentence in the paragraph. Also observe that the writer captured the readers' attention by relating the topic to the readers' own experiences.

Your dog probably understands a lot of what you say, but have you ever wished your dog could talk back to you? You and your dog will never have a conversation in human language. However, scientists who study animal behavior tell us that dogs do use sounds, their faces, and their bodies to communicate with other dogs and with humans.

KEY 5

## Draft the Body of Your Paper

The main part of your paper is called "the body." To write this important part of your paper, include only *relevant* information, or information that gets to the point. Organize your ideas in a logical order—one
that makes sense—and provide enough details—facts and examples—
to support the points you want to make.

### Relevance

You presented the main idea of your paper in the thesis statement. In
the body, every single paragraph must support that main idea. If any
paragraph in your paper does not, in some way, back up the main idea
expressed in your thesis statement, it is not relevant, which means it
doesn't have a purpose and shouldn't be there.

Each paragraph also has a main idea of its own. That main idea is
stated in a topic sentence, either at the beginning or somewhere else in
the paragraph. Just as every paragraph in your paper supports your
thesis statement, every sentence in each paragraph supports the main
idea of that paragraph by providing facts or examples that back up that
main idea. If a sentence does not support the main idea of the paragraph, it is not relevant and should be left out.

### Support

A paper that makes claims or states ideas without backing them up
with facts or clarifying them with examples won't mean much to
readers. Make sure you provide enough supporting details for all your
ideas. And remember that a paragraph can't contain just one sentence.
A paragraph needs at least two or more sentences to be complete. If a
paragraph has only one or two sentences, you probably haven't provided enough support for your main idea. Or, if you have trouble finding

the main idea, maybe you don't have one. In that case, you can make the sentences part of another paragraph or leave them out.

### Logical order

Arrange the paragraphs in the body of your paper in an order that makes sense, so that each main idea follows logically from the previous one. Likewise, arrange the sentences in each paragraph in a logical order.

If you carefully organized your notes and made your outline, your ideas will fall into place naturally as you write your draft. The main ideas, which are building blocks of each section or each paragraph in your paper, come from the Roman-numeral headings in your outline. The supporting details under each of those main ideas come from the capital-letter headings. In a shorter paper, the capital-letter headings may become sentences that include supporting details, which come from the Arabic numerals in your outline. In a longer paper, the capital-letter headings may become paragraphs of their own, which contain sentences with the supporting details, which come from the Arabic numerals in your outline.

### Transitions

In addition to keeping your ideas in logical order, *transitions* are another way to guide readers from one idea to another. Transitions are words such as *therefore*, *however*, *in addition*, and *on the other hand*. They help readers see the relationships between your ideas. Without transitions, writing is hard to follow, and it sounds choppy. Here is an example of a passage that needs a transition:

> When a dog wags its tail, it may be expressing happiness. It may be showing aggression.

K
E
Y
5

Here is the same passage with a transition:

> When a dog wags its tail, it may be expressing happiness. On the other hand, it may be showing aggression.

## Draft Your Conclusion

Every good paper ends with a strong concluding paragraph. To write a good conclusion, sum up the main points in your paper. To write an even better conclusion, include a sentence or two that helps the reader answer the question, "So what?" or "Why does all this matter?" If you choose to include one or more "So What?" sentences, remember that you still need to support any point you make with facts or examples. Remember, too, that this is not the place to introduce new ideas from "out of the blue." Make sure that everything you write in your conclusion refers to what you've already written in the body of your paper.

### INSIDE SECRET

## It's Only a Draft

A blank sheet of white paper can make even an experienced writer nervous. If you're experiencing a touch of blank-paper fright, say these words to yourself: "It's only a draft!" No one but you sees what you write at this stage. For now, focus on getting your thoughts down on paper. You can improve and polish it later.

## Cite Your Sources

Chapter 2 talked about giving credit to the source of any facts or ideas you use in your paper. Giving credit to a source is called *citing* that source. Another way to say "citing sources" is "documenting information." Either way, your paper must include information about where you found your facts and ideas.

## To Cite or Not to Cite

When you appropriately cite your sources, you show your readers that you are knowledgeable about your topic. How do you know when to cite a certain source? After all, you don't want to document information that everyone already knows. For example, if you mention in your paper that Washington, D.C., is the capital of the United States, you don't need to cite a source. The way to know if you need to cite a source is to ask yourself this question: "If I don't cite a source for this fact or idea, will readers think that I came up with it myself?" If you still aren't sure of the answer, then follow this basic rule: When in doubt, cite.

## How to Cite Sources

Some high school teachers and college professors want students to cite sources in *footnotes* or *endnotes*. Footnotes are notes that appear at the bottom of each page, and endnotes belong at the end of the paper. To create the notes, you assign a number, beginning with 1, for each fact or idea to document. Then, following a special style, you match each number with a note that tells the source of the information. All of these notes appear at the end of the paper, or at the bottom of the page, in numerical order.

Your teacher probably prefers a less complicated method—putting a *source note* in parentheses right after the relevant information. The source note needs to include two things: the last name of the author of the book where you found the information and the number of the page where the information appeared. For example, a source note for a fact that was found on page 48 of a book written by Karen Johnson looks like this: *(Johnson, 48)*. If you use another book by an author with the same last name, include the author's first name as well—*(Dana Johnson, 48).* If you used another book by the same author, include the title of the book—*(Dana Johnson,* Volcanoes, *48).*

The end of your paper includes a *bibliography*—a list of all the sources you used, with complete information about each one. The reader can look there to find out more about the sources you cite in your source notes.

## Choose a Title

The title is the first thing readers see when they look at your paper. So why bring up titles after going over drafting the introduction, body, and conclusion of the paper? The reason is simple: Drafting your paper may give you ideas for a title. Here are two rules for choosing a title:

1. Keep it short.
2. Make sure it lets readers know what your paper is about.

The title for the paper on dog communication, for example, could simply be "Dog Communication." If you want to tell a little more, you can add a subtitle, separated from the main title by a colon. For example, your title could be "Dog Communication: Understanding What Dogs Have to Say."

Some students put lots of effort into coming up with a clever title. It's a bonus if your title can capture your readers' attention, but it's a mistake—and a waste of time—to use a title that's too cute. "Woofs and Wags: Dog Language Made Easy" is not a good title because it creates confusion. A title that uses a pun, such as "Tails Dogs Tell," is also unclear. A research paper is a serious piece of writing, so you don't want the title to give readers—including your teacher—the impression that your paper is a "puff piece."

Ready Set.

# REVIEW

## Practice Writing

1. Choose a title for each of the following research papers:

- In social studies, you are studying the Middle Ages in Europe. Your paper is about knights. It tells how a person became a knight and what the life of a knight was like.
- In science, you are studying plants. Your paper is about plants of the desert and how they survive in a hot, dry environment.
- In English language arts, you are reading about Greek myths. Your paper is about the religion of the ancient Greeks. It tells about the gods they believed in and how they worshipped them.

2. Add transitions to each of the following passages to make them smooth and logical:

- Dogs come in many shapes, sizes, and colors, from Great Danes and Saint Bernards to Chihuahuas, beagles, and dachshunds. All the different breeds of dogs come from the same original ancestor.
- These days, most people live well into their 70s or 80s. Once, the average life expectancy for a human being was less than 30 years.
- Modern cities usually have many skyscrapers, often close to a thousand feet tall. New York's Flatiron Building, finished in 1903, was thought of as amazing. It was 23 stories tall.

KEY 5

## KEY 6

# REVISE AND EDIT YOUR DRAFT

✓ **Check Each Part**

✓ **Aim for Excellence**

✓ **Proofread**

✓ **Take Pride in Your Bibliography**

*You've come a long way, but you're not finished yet!*

You started out without knowing what you were going to write about, and now you have in your hand, or on your screen, pages filled with information. What you have is a first draft—and no one's first draft is perfect. To turn that draft into a finished paper you feel proud to hand in, read it again from beginning to end, and then make some improvements. This process is called **revising and editing.** To see an example of a revised and edited research paper, complete with a list of its sources and note cards, look at Appendix B at the back of this book.

## Check Each Part

The first step in the revising and editing process is to start reading your draft from the beginning and make sure that each part—the introduction, body, and conclusion—does the job it's supposed to do. For each part of your draft, ask yourself the questions on the following checklist. If your answer to any question is "no," make the revisions necessary to change your answer to "yes."

### Check Your Introduction

- Does your introduction capture your readers' attention?

- Does your introduction contain a thesis statement that clearly states the main idea of your paper?

### Check the Body of Your Paper

- Does every paragraph in the body of your paper support your thesis statement?

- Does every paragraph state a main idea in a topic sentence?

- Does every sentence in each paragraph support the main idea of the paragraph?

- Have you taken out any information that is irrelevant, or beside the point?

- Do your paragraphs provide enough support for the main idea of your paper as it appears in your thesis statement?

- In every paragraph, do you provide enough support for the main idea expressed in its topic sentence?

- Do your paragraphs flow in a logical order?

- Do the sentences in each paragraph flow in a logical order?

- Have you used transitions?

## Check Your Conclusion

- Does your conclusion sum up the main points in your paper?

- Does your conclusion help readers answer the question, "So what?"

## Aim for Excellence

Your paper is really shaping up now. But a truly excellent paper has to do even more than get a yes answer to every question in the preceding checklists. It needs to be *well written.* In other words, it has to sound good and be free of errors in spelling, grammar, and punctuation.

## Spell Check

If you're writing your paper on a computer, of course you can use the spell-checker function. That part of your word processing program picks up most spelling errors. But it doesn't catch all of them. For example, if you've typed the word *though* incorrectly by leaving out the letter *h* at the beginning, the word comes out as *tough.* Your spell checker does not catch that as a mistake because *tough* is a word. So whether you work on a computer or not, be sure to read through your paper—word for word—to correct any spelling errors. If you aren't sure how to spell a word, look it up.

## Check Grammar and Punctuation

A good knowledge of the rules of language helps you make sure your paper is free of grammar and punctuation errors. You can use the following lists to help you avoid common errors. However, if you have specific questions about the rules of grammar, usage, and mechanics, your language arts textbook explains all of the rules and offers further examples.

K
E
Y

6

## Sentences

Make sure each of your sentences is complete, which means that each sentence has a subject and a verb.

> Wrong: Climates farther from the equator usually cooler.
> Right: Climates farther from the equator are usually cooler.

## Subject-verb agreement

A verb must always agree in number with its subject. In other words, if a subject is singular, the verb must be singular; if the subject is plural, the verb must be plural. If the subject of a sentence is the word *each*, the subject is singular even though it may sound as if it were plural. This means the verb is singular too.

> Wrong: Each of the players begin with a warm-up.
> Right: Each of the players begins with a warm-up.

## Using pronouns correctly

A *pronoun* always refers to a noun that has already been mentioned. A writer must always make it clear which noun the pronoun is referring to. In the first sentence below, a reader can't tell whether the pronoun *it* refers to Athens or Sparta.

> Wrong: One way in which ancient Athens differed from ancient
>     Sparta is that it gave women more equality.
> Right: One way in which ancient Athens differed from ancient
>     Sparta is that Sparta gave women more equality.

Another common error is using subject and object pronouns incorrectly. When a pronoun is the subject of a sentence, always use *I*, *she*, *he*, *we*, or *they*. When a pronoun is a direct object, indirect object, or object of a preposition, always use *me*, *her*, *him*, *us*, or *them*.

Wrong: Him and the president were both elected for two terms.

Right: He and the president were both elected for two terms.

Some writers tend to think that subject pronouns such as *he* and *I* always sound more correct than object pronouns such as *him* and *me*, but that is not true.

Wrong: The conversation between he and I was interesting.

Right: The conversation between him and me was interesting.

## *Misplaced and dangling modifiers*

Always be sure that your readers can tell which word is being described by another word or phrase. In the first of the sentences below, the reader might think that *With its powerful wings* describes *human* instead of *bird.* You can avoid this error by placing the modifying word or phrase as close as possible to the word it describes.

Wrong: With its powerful wings, a human cannot fly like a bird.

Right: With its powerful wings, a bird can fly, but a human cannot.

### Irregular verbs

Most verbs in English take *-ed* in the past tense. However, some verbs have irregular past-tense forms. Be sure you know those forms and write them correctly. Here are a few examples:

| Wrong: | Right: |
|---|---|
| sleeped | slept |
| leaved | left |
| thinked | thought |
| buyed | bought |
| sended | sent |

### Missing commas

Placing a comma after an introductory phrase or clause makes writing clear and easy to understand. Leaving out a comma can confuse your readers.

Wrong: Although some animals hibernate in the winter winter is a time of activity for many animals.

Right: Although some animals hibernate in the winter, winter is a time of activity for many animals.

Using commas where they are not necessary can also be confusing, so try to pay attention to whether your sentences include commas too often.

## Avoid Repetition

If you find that in your paper you have used the same word over and over, replace the repeated word with another one that has a similar meaning. Too much repetition makes writing sound boring.

Another kind of repetition to avoid is using the same type of sentence too many times in a row. This can make writing sound boring, too. Varying your sentences makes your writing livelier and more interesting to readers.

In the examples below, the writer revised her work by beginning the first sentence with a dependent clause instead of the subject. She also avoided repeating the word *city* by using a synonym, *municipality*.

> Boring: Lake City was founded in 1836. It has a population of 30,800 people. It was named Lake City because it is located near a lake called Beaver Lake.

> More Variety: Founded in 1836, Lake City has a population of 30,800 people. The municipality got its name from the lake near which it is located.

## INSIDE SECRET

### Use Your Electronic Thesaurus

One way to liven up your writing is to avoid repeating the same word too many times. If you're writing on a computer, your word processing program probably has its own thesaurus. Use it to find a synonym for a word you've been using too often.

KEY 6

## Break Up Paragraphs That Are Too Long

If you've written a paragraph that seems to go on forever or that is much longer than the other paragraphs in your paper, consider breaking it up into two shorter ones. Overly long paragraphs can lose readers' attention. If you do break a long paragraphs into two shorter ones, be sure each one has its own main idea and topic sentence.

# WRITING IT RIGHT

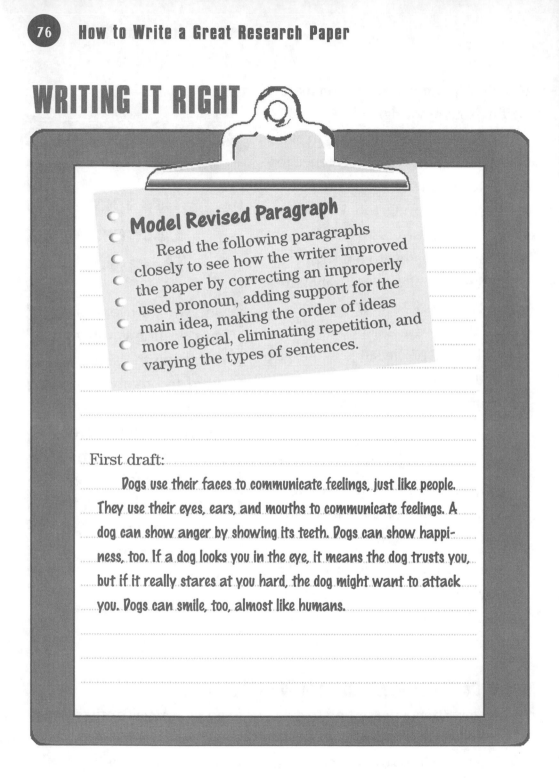

## Model Revised Paragraph

Read the following paragraphs closely to see how the writer improved the paper by correcting an improperly used pronoun, adding support for the main idea, making the order of ideas more logical, eliminating repetition, and varying the types of sentences.

First draft:

Dogs use their faces to communicate feelings, just like people. They use their eyes, ears, and mouths to communicate feelings. A dog can show anger by showing its teeth. Dogs can show happiness, too. If a dog looks you in the eye, it means the dog trusts you, but if it really stares at you hard, the dog might want to attack you. Dogs can smile, too, almost like humans.

# WRITING IT RIGHT

Revised paragraph:

Like people, dogs use their faces to communicate. Their eyes, ears, and mouths can tell a lot about how they feel. If a dog looks you in the eye, it probably trusts you, but if it really stares at you hard, the dog might want to attack you. Ears held back mean that a dog is angry. Another way a dog shows anger is by showing its teeth. A dog that is staring at you, showing its teeth, growling or snarling, and holding its ears back is <u>really</u> angry. But dogs show happiness with their faces too. They sometimes show they are happy and content by pulling their lips back and opening their mouths a little without showing their teeth. That expression is similar to a human smile.

KEY 6

## Proofread

After revising and editing your draft, put it away for a day or two—if you have time, of course. Then look at it again. Mistakes that you might have missed pop out at you after you and your paper have had a little vacation from each other. At this point, do your final fixes, making sure everything is as good as you can make it. If you've written your paper on a computer, print it out for proofreading. Often, writers see mistakes on paper that they miss on a computer screen. After you proofread, you can type in your corrections.

Another way to catch mistakes and to find areas that still need improvement is to read your work aloud to yourself. Hearing the words in your paper is a particularly good way to call attention to problems such as repetition, improper use of pronouns, and mistakes in subject-verb agreement.

Another good idea is to ask someone else to read your paper and give you feedback. A pair of eyes besides your own can pick up details that you

**INSIDE SECRET**

### Proofreading Marks

As you proofread your first draft, your changes and corrections may include adding (inserting), deleting (taking out), and moving letters, words, punctuation marks, and whole sentences. If you're working on a computer, you can make your corrections right on the screen. If you're working on paper, using proofreading marks makes your job easier.

*(Continued)*

may miss. Your reader, whether a classmate or an adult, should not change your paper. He or she should only suggest additional changes and improvements, which you can make yourself.

Here are some of the marks that seasoned writers find most useful:

¶ = Begin a new paragraph

∧ = add, or insert

≤ or ≥ = move words you've circled

ℓ = take out, or delete

## Take Pride in Your Bibliography

Your bibliography is a list of all the sources you used for your research paper. Creating your bibliography is simple because you have all the information you need. You recorded it on the source cards you made when you were just beginning your research. In your bibliography, list only those sources that you actually used in your paper. (That means you may not use all of your source cards.)

A bibliography usually appears at the end of a paper on its own separate page. All bibliography entries—books, periodicals, Web sites, and nontext sources such radio broadcasts—are listed together in alphabetical order. Books and articles are alphabetized by the author's last name.

Most teachers suggest that you follow a standard style for listing different types of sources. If your teacher asks you to use a different form, however, follow his or her instructions. Take pride in your bibliography. It represents some of the most important work you've done for your research paper—and using proper form shows that you are a serious and careful researcher.

## Bibliography Entry for a Book

A bibliography entry for a book begins with the author's name, which is written in this order: last name, comma, first name, period. After the author's name comes the title of the book. If you are handwriting your bibliography, underline each title. If you are working on a computer, put the book title in italicized type. Be sure to capitalize the words in the title correctly, exactly as they are written in the book itself. Following the title is the city where the book was published, followed by a colon, the name of the publisher, a comma, the date published, and a period. Here is an example:

> White, Nancy. *Why Do Dogs Do That?* New York: Scholastic, 1995.

## Bibliography Entry for a Periodical

A bibliography entry for a periodical differs slightly in form from a bibliography entry for a book. For a magazine article, start with the author's last name first, followed by a comma, then the first name and a period. Next, write the title of the article in quotation marks, and include a period (or other closing punctuation) inside the closing quotation mark. The title of the magazine is next, underlined or in italic type, depending on whether you are handwriting or using a computer, followed by a period. The date and year, followed by a colon and the pages on which the article appeared, come last. Here is an example:

> Bascom, Elizabeth. "Tail Talk." *Pet World Magazine.* April 11, 1999: 22–26.

For a newspaper article, the letter before the page number refers to the section of the newspaper where the article appeared. For example, section A might be the main news section, section B might be the local news section, and section C may be the science section.

> Ryan, Elizabeth. "The Language of Barking." *The New York Times*. April 24, 2001: C-18.

## Bibliography Entry for a Nonprint Source

For sources such as Web sites or radio broadcasts, include the information a reader needs to find the source or to know where and when you found it. Always begin with the last name of the author, broadcaster, person you interviewed, and so on. Here is an example of a bibliography for a Web site:

> Dodman, Dr. Nicholas. "The Body Language of Dogs." http://www.petplace.com/Articles/(04/11/03).

Here is an example of a bibliography entry for a television show:

> Public Broadcasting System. "What's That Animal Saying?" June 19, 2003, 8:00–9:00 P.M.

K
E
Y
6

Ready Set...

# REVIEW

## Practice Revising

1. The following paragraph comes from the first draft of a research paper about penguins. Look for ways to improve the paragraph. Then write your own revised version of the paragraph. Here are some hints: You need to make at least three corrections: Correct a verb that does not agree with its subject, add a missing comma, and revise at least one sentence to add variety.

> The emperor penguins have an unusual way of taking care of their eggs. Each of the female penguins lay just one egg. Then she goes to sea. The male stays on land and keeps the egg warm by holding it on his feet. All the males in the group huddle together to keep warm. They take turns staying on the inside of the huddle, where it is warm, and on the outside, where it is colder. They live on stored body fat for the entire 72 days it takes for the eggs to hatch. They lose about half their body weight. When the chicks are born the females return to care for them.

2. Some of the following sentences contain errors that should be corrected. Make the appropriate corrections where necessary. One sentence is correct as written.

- The soldiers of Washington's army was often short of ammunition and warm clothing.
- Although many kinds of plant life are able to manufacture all of their own food, some species rely on nourishment from other sources.
- Napoleon Bonaparte conquered many nations, but he spends the last years of his life confined to a tiny, barren island.
- Between you and I, I have never been very good at long division.

# PRESENT YOUR PAPER

✓ **Neatness Counts**

✓ **Using Visuals**

✓ **Presenting in Public**

*You've completed your research paper! Just one final task remains—preparing to present your paper.*

**N**ow you can breathe a huge sigh of relief and pat yourself on the back. You probably plan to turn in your work in printed or handwritten form, but you also may be making an oral presentation. However you plan to present your paper, do your best to show it in its best light. You've put a great deal of work and thought into this assignment, so you want your paper to look and sound its best. After completing all of the preparation for your paper, you may want to evaluate your own performance by using the self-evaluation chart (Appendix C) at the end of the book.

## Neatness Counts

What you say and how you say it are the things that really count. But when your teacher or another reader is looking at your writing, he or she can't help letting how the paper looks influence the way he or she judges your paper. First impressions are important, so be sure your work looks neat.

## Using Visuals

Illustrations and other visuals can make your paper livelier and more interesting—if they actually add something to the text. Don't use them just for decoration because that gives your paper a babyish look. However, if you mention something in your paper that might be unfamiliar to readers—a certain plant or animal, for example—a picture helps readers understand what you are saying. Also, if you include complicated information that a chart or graph can clarify, try to supply a visual that makes your point clearer.

Even if you don't consider yourself a talented artist, you can create simple illustrations of your own. You also can photocopy photographs or drawings, in color or in black and white, or copy

### INSIDE SECRET

## Making Last-Minute Corrections

If you've handwritten your paper and have to make one or two last-minute corrections on your final copy, neatly draw a single line through the word or words you want to delete. Use a *caret* (∧) to show that you are inserting one or more words. Carefully write the inserted words above the caret. Make corrections neatly and clearly.

# WRITING IT RIGHT

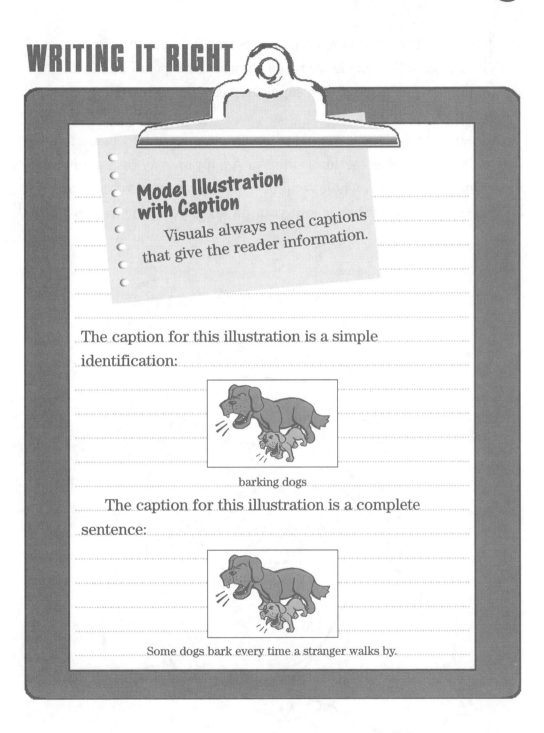

## Model Illustration with Caption

Visuals always need captions that give the reader information.

The caption for this illustration is a simple identification:

barking dogs

The caption for this illustration is a complete sentence:

Some dogs bark every time a stranger walks by.

KEY 7

and paste art files on a computer—as long as you cite the sources of the illustrations. You can leave room to paste or tape an illustration within the text, or place it on a separate page that immediately follows the text that mentions it.

A visual always needs a caption—a line or two of text beneath it that tells the reader something about it. A caption may be a simple identifying phrase or a whole sentence. Whichever type of caption you choose, be consistent throughout your paper. If you provide three illus-

trations, for example, the captions for all three must be either complete sentences or short identifying phrases—not a mix of both.

## Presenting in Public

All you have to do now is hand your research paper in to your teacher— unless you plan to present it to your classmates or another audience. Even if you have a photographic memory, your voice naturally projects to the back of any room, and you really enjoy performing before an audience, you still need to organize the way you present your thoughts. But if you're like most people, you need help remembering what you want to say. Many people get nervous in front of an audience. However, if you prepare properly, your talk can go smoothly and be a positive experience.

### Using Note Cards As You Present

Why not just stand in front of the class and read your paper out loud? If you do that, you might as well make copies of your paper and hand them out to your audience. When people come to hear an oral presentation, they want to listen to an interesting speaker. They want to hear your voice and see your

---

**INSIDE SECRET**

### Overcoming Stage Fright

The best way to overcome stage fright is to be well prepared. Take time to practice, especially in front of a mirror. Present your paper to one or two friends or relatives, and ask them to suggest ways to improve your presentation. Then try it again. The more you practice, the more confident you'll feel when standing in front of the class.

KEY 7

facial expressions, which give them a better understanding of what you are saying.

Making eye contact is an important way of holding your audience's attention, but you can't do that when you are holding your paper in front of your face. On the other hand, you want to be sure to mention all of the major points in your paper—without getting offtrack on the details. How can you do that? The answer is to use note cards.

Go through your paper and note each main point on a separate index card. Don't write out whole sentences because that's reading exactly what's on your paper. On each card, write a few words that remind you of one main idea. Then, for each main idea, jot down a few additional words that remind you of your supporting details. Write big, and use a dark pen or pencil—or even a marker—so you won't need to hold your cards close to your eyes to read them. Remember, the important thing is to get across your ideas (not deliver your paper word for word as you wrote it).

When you present, hold your cards in your hand or keep them on a desk in front of you. Glance down occasionally to consult your notes, but make sure you look up at your audience again as quickly as possible to maintain eye contact. When you've finished with a card, put it on the bottom of the pile or turn it over onto a second pile that's beside the cards you still plan to use.

## Speaking Slowly and Loudly

When you give an oral presentation, speak so that your audience can hear you easily and understand everything you say. Inexperienced speakers, especially if they are nervous, tend to race through their talks and let their voice drop. How can the audience appreciate what you're saying if no one can hear you? You can avoid these pitfalls by speaking even more slowly and more loudly than you think is necessary when you practice. If someone listens to your practice presentation, be sure to ask him or her if you are speaking at a comfortable speed and volume.

Now that you've done all that, you can feel proud. You've taken on a big job and seen it through from beginning to end. Take a deep breath and feel good about what you've accomplished. Congratulations!

*Ready Set.*

# REVIEW

## Practice Presenting Your Paper

1. Choose one of the following visuals to create for a paper on a topic you want to write about. Write a full-sentence caption for your visual.

   - an original illustration
   - a photocopied illustration from a book
   - a chart
   - a graph

2. Practice presenting your research paper out loud before you actually present it in class. You can do this yourself, in front of a mirror, using a tape recorder, videotape, or camcorder, so that you can listen and/or watch yourself afterward. Or if you can arrange it, try your practice presentation in front of a small audience of friends or family members. If you do that with a classmate or two, you can take turns presenting your papers for one another.

   Afterward, you can share notes and make suggestions for ways to improve your presentation technique.

KEY 7

# Appendix A

## Scheduling Form

When you get your research assignment, use this form to schedule your work. It can help you keep track of what you've done, what you still have to do, and how much time you have to do it. You may change the dates as you work, but remember that the final due date stays the same.

| Task | Date I Plan to Finish | Date Finished |
|---|---|---|
| Find a topic | | |
| Do preliminary research | | |
| Complete source cards | | |
| Complete research and note cards | | |
| Create outline | | |
| Write first draft | | |
| Revise and edit first draft | | |
| Prepare presentation | | |
| Final due date: | | |

# Appendix B

## Model Research Paper

Please note that requirements for each research paper may vary greatly. Many research papers you are asked to write will be much longer than the one you see here. The model paper shows you how the basic format works. Of course, you'll want to meet your teacher's requirements for length, following the assignment you're given for each research paper.

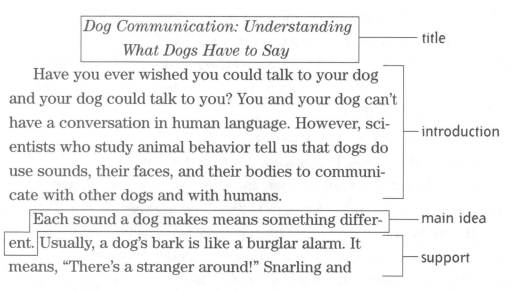

*Dog Communication: Understanding What Dogs Have to Say* ——— title

Have you ever wished you could talk to your dog and your dog could talk to you? You and your dog can't have a conversation in human language. However, scientists who study animal behavior tell us that dogs do use sounds, their faces, and their bodies to communicate with other dogs and with humans. ——— introduction

Each sound a dog makes means something different. ——— main idea

Usually, a dog's bark is like a burglar alarm. It means, "There's a stranger around!" Snarling and ——— support

growling mean that a dog is angry. Dogs also whimper
or whine sometimes if they are unhappy or feeling sick.
Some dogs howl when they hear a fire siren or someone practicing a trumpet or violin. When a dog howls,   — support
it is acting like a wolf. Wolves howl to one another to
keep the wolf pack together. A howling dog probably
thinks it is answering the call of its pack *(Ryan, C-18)*.

    Like people, dogs use their faces to communicate.
Their eyes, ears, and mouths can tell a lot about how
they feel. If a dog looks you in the eye, it probably
trusts you, but if it really stares at you hard, the dog
might want to attack you. Ears held back mean that a
dog is angry. Another way a dog shows anger is by
showing its teeth. A dog that is staring at you, showing
its teeth, growling or snarling, and holding its ears back
is *really* angry. But dogs show happiness with their     — transition
faces, too. They sometimes show they are happy and
content by pulling their lips back and opening their
mouths a little without showing their teeth. This
expression is similar to a human smile *(Morris, 68)*.     — cite sources

    You can tell a lot about how a dog is feeling by its     — main idea
body. For example, if a dog's tail is up, the dog is
happy, but if the tail is very straight and stiff, the dog
might be angry. If the tail is hanging down loosely, the
dog feels OK, but if the tail is down and close to its     — support
rump, the dog is unhappy. A dog puts its tail all the way
between its hind legs if it is sick or in pain. When dogs
wag their tails in wide, loose wags, that's a friendly
sign. But short, quick, stiff wags can mean the dog     — transition
wants to fight. Another way a dog can show it wants to

fight is to make the hair along its back stand up. If a dog *doesn't* want to fight, it rolls over on its back. One of the cutest kinds of dog body language is called the *play-bow*. A dog puts its front paws out with its chest almost touching the ground, sticks its rear end up in the air, and wags its tail. This means, "Come and play with me!" Licking your hand or face is one of the nicest things a dog can do. It shows that the dog loves you the way a puppy loves a mother dog *(White, 37)*.

Even if you don't have your own dog, knowing about dog communication can be very useful. For example, if a dog is staring at you with its ears back and its teeth showing, you should not stare back. Just back away slowly. If you hear your dog barking, you should go to the door and see who is there instead of telling the dog to be quiet. And if your dog is inviting you to play, you can be her best friend by accepting the invitation.

— conclusion

Bibliography

George, Jean Graighead. *How to Talk to Your Dog.* New York: Harper Collins Publishers, 2000.

Mendel, Dr. Wilma. Interviewed 8/10/03 at 300 Central Avenue, Clearview, Ohio, 3:30 P.M.

Morris, Desmond. *Dogwatching.* New York: Crown Publishers, 1986.

Ryan, Elizabeth. "The Language of Barking." *The New York Times,* April 24, 2001: C-18.

White, Nancy. *Why Do Dogs Do That?* New York: Scholastic, 1995.

## Bibliography Cards

#1

White, Nancy. Why Do Dogs Do That? New York: Scholastic, 1995.

#2

George, Jean Craighead. How to Talk to Your Dog. New York: Harper Collins, 2000.

#3

Morris, Desmond. Dogwatching. New York: Crown, 1986.

#4

Ryan, Elizabeth. "The Language of Barking." The New York Times, April 24, 2001: C-18.

#5

Mendel, Dr. Wilma. Interviewed 8/10 at 300 Central Avenue, Clearview, Ohio, 3:30 P.M.

# Note Cards

| #4                                Barking |
|---|
| Different barks have different meanings |
|  |
|  |
|  |

| #3                                Barking |
|---|
| p. 17 |
| Barking an alarm: "There is something strange happening over here. Be alert!" |
|  |
|  |

| #3                                Snarling |
|---|
| p. 18 |
| Snarling and growling—angry |
|  |
|  |
|  |

| #1                    Whining and whimpering |
|---|
| p. 16 |
| Whining and whimpering—dog is unhappy. Might be sick |
|  |
|  |

#3                                                  Howling
p. 21

Fire siren, sound of trumpet or violin—
can make some dogs howl

---

#3                                                  Howling
p. 21

Howling—acting like wolf. Wolves howl
to each other to keep pack together

---

#2                                           Face expression
p. 15

Dog looks you in the eye—trusts you

---

#2                                                     Eyes
p. 15

Stares at you hard—might want to
attack

#2                                    Ear position
p. 4

Ears held back—angry

---

#1                                           Teeth
p. 12

Showing teeth—angry

---

#1                                            Face
p. 17

Staring, showing teeth, ears back—very
angry

---

#1                                    Face (smile)
p. 15

Pulling back lips and opening mouth a
little with teeth showing, but not much.
Means dog is happy.

#2　　　　　　　　　　　　　　　　　Tail
p. 14

Tail up means happy

#2　　　　　　　　　　　　　　　　　Tail
p. 14

Straight up and stiff means angry

#2　　　　　　　　　　　　　　　　　Tail
p. 14

Hanging down loosely—feels OK

#2　　　　　　　　　　　　　　　　　Tail
p. 14

Tail down close to rump means dog is
unhappy

#2                                    Tail
p. 14

Tail all the way down and between legs
means dog might be sick or in pain

---

#1                              Tail wagging
p. 6

Loose, loose wags—friendly

---

#1                              Tail wagging
p. 6

Quick, stiff wags—dog might want to
fight with another dog

---

#1                              Hair on back
p. 12

Hair on back standing up means dogs
want to fight. Angry.

# 3                                      Rolling on back
p. 43

Rolling over on back means dog is saying
"I give up." "I don't want to fight."

---

#3                                           Play-bow
p. 38

Front paws down, chest near grond, rear
end up is the "play-bow"

---

#1                                            Licking
p. 9

Licking hand or face—puppies lick mother dog. Means "I love you."

---

#5                              How to treat angry dog

If dog is staring, ears back, showing
teeth, DON'T stare back. Back away
slowly.

---

#5                                What to do if dog barks

Go to door and see who is there. Don't
scold dog for barking. Dog is just doing its
job.

# Appendix C

## Self-Evaluation: Learning from the Research Experience

The beginning of this book claims that you can gain these four things from writing a research paper:

- experience writing research papers (so that the next time you do it, you'll know how)

- knowledge about a topic that interests you (so you'll become an expert)

- experience doing research (so that you'll always be able to find information you need)

- satisfaction and pride (in seeing a task through from beginning to end)

Now that you've completed your paper, think about what you have learned and what you have gained. Have you gained the kind of experience or knowledge described in each of the four points above? Rank each one on a scale of 1 to 4, with 4 standing for an enthusiastic yes answer and 1 for a not really. Look at any ranking below a 3 and ask yourself the question, "What happened?" Try to figure out why you didn't learn as much as you could have in this particular area. Next time around, see if you can do better.

Use the following chart to evaluate your experience. For each statement in the first column, put a check mark under 1, 2, 3, or 4 to show your ranking.

| | 1<br>Not really | 2<br>Sort of | 3<br>Pretty good | 4<br>Yes! |
|---|---|---|---|---|
| Now I know how to write a research paper. | | | | |
| I've become an expert on my topic. | | | | |
| I can use my research skills to find information I need. | | | | |
| I am proud of the job I did on this paper. | | | | |

# Index